Houdini's Tour of Australia

Leann Richards

Houdini's Tour of Australia

Houdini's Tour of Australia
ISBN 978 1 74027 396 1
Copyright © Leann Richards 2006

First published 2006
Reprinted 2018

GINNINDERRA PRESS
PO Box 3461 Port Adelaide 5015
www.ginninderrapress.com.au

Contents

Arrival	7
Melbourne	10
The first performance in Melbourne	11
The committee man	16
The Yarra dive	17
The milk can escape	21
The Melbourne challenges	24
Sceptic	31
First flight	32
Houdini's Arrival in Sydney	41
The Sydney Tivoli performance	42
Autumn in Australia	47
The dive into the Dom Baths	50
The Sydney challenges	54
Flying in Sydney	58
Farewell	63
Sources	64
Ephemera	66

Arrival

In 1909, Australian theatre owner Harry Rickards met Harry Houdini. Rickards offered the escapologist $2,000 a week, including travel time, to visit Australia the next year. Houdini accepted. As a result, on 5 February 1910, Harry Houdini arrived in Adelaide. His wife Bess, assistants Franz Kukol and James Vickery, mechanic Mr Brassac and a Voisin aeroplane accompanied him.

Houdini's arrival was announced in *The Magic Mirror*, the journal of the Australian Society of Magicians, in a simple sentence:

> Houdini arrived Adelaide, February 5th per RMS *Malwa*.

Reporters must have been waiting for him at the dock, as by Monday 7 February, The local Adelaide paper, *The Advertiser*, had his first Australian interview in print. The interview was titled 'The Handcuff King'. In the first paragraph it stated that Houdini had 'come to the Commonwealth under engagement to Mr Harry Rickards'.

Houdini either introduced himself as 'legal name, Harry "Handcuff" Houdini' or the paper dubbed him as such. Either way, this legal entity was described as being born in Appleton Wisconsin on 6 April 1874 (he was actually born on 24 March), which made him thirty-five years old when he first set foot on Australian soil. Houdini told the reporter that

> After my Australian engagement I have another 18 months of professional work and then I shall have finished.

He was establishing a theme that would be repeated throughout his stay – retirement. Of course he never retired and worked almost ceaselessly until a few days before his death.

Harry described himself as

> The original handcuff king... I have heard that there have been quite a number of handcuff kings out here.

He added that he no longer performed as many handcuff escapes as he once did 'because it has become old'. He stated that he was performing more novelties, like straitjacket escapes. Thus Houdini built on his handcuff reputation in order to enhance the new parts of his performance.

The handcuff king, who no longer did handcuff escapes, then discussed the experience of the long voyage. He had suffered from seasickness. It was one of Houdini's weaknesses. He told the reporter that he had lost a stone (about six kilograms) in weight during the voyage. Houdini must have been feeling a mixture of relief and wretchedness as he spoke to reporters after the ship had docked. Yet the business of promoting Houdini had to continue. He told reporters that he had once dived ninety-six feet (29.26 metres) manacled and into ice-covered water in the middle of winter. He added that a hole had to be cut in the ice so that he could dive into it. Houdini stated that he had 'hardened his system to the cold', was an 'all the year round bather' and could stay underwater 'at freezing point with ease for from two to three minutes'. Thus he emphasised his great physical abilities and athletic achievements, which indicated that it was these talents that he relied upon for his act.

He did have reservations about performing such a dive in Australia:

> I hear though that you have sharks in your waters. Perhaps it would not do for me to take the risk out here for the sharks might get me.

It was typical of Houdini to pepper his conversations and interviews with stories of his adventures. Houdini had collected certificates verifying his escapes from police chiefs around the world. He collected similar certificates about his aviation feats whilst in Australia. Finally he added that he would perform in Adelaide. He did not perform in that city. He was limited to performing in Melbourne and Sydney.

Melbourne in fact was his next stop. He was due to start his season at the New Opera House in Bourke Street on Monday 7 February. Harry Rickards had arranged it, and Houdini was about to fulfil his contractual promise. He was not, however, about to undertake another sea journey. The trip to Melbourne, 514 miles (827.2 kilometres) of it, was taken by the Overlander or Melbourne Express train. It was a long monotonous journey of approximately seventeen and a half hours, over flat, often deserted countryside. Houdini arrived in Melbourne, fit and ready to work, without the pangs of seasickness standing in his way.

Melbourne

Houdini arrived in Melbourne on Sunday 6 February 1910. He was a short, sturdy man with a broad forehead and grey eyes. He spoke with an American accent, which was tinged with a slight eastern European twang. He was just a month from his thirty-sixth birthday and had dark hair sprinkled with grey. He was not young, yet not too old, a man in his prime middle years, fit, muscular, and charismatic.

Houdini's assistants and his wife, Bess, accompanied him. She was a small, stocky lady, with a round, heavily made up face surrounded by dark hair. By this time the Houdinis had been married for sixteen years. Bess was described as 'a neat little figure', or 'the pretty young lady'. She was always mentioned in relation to her husband and never as an individual with her own opinions. Descriptions of her conformed to the conservative ideals of women held at the time.

Bess, however, was instrumental to her husband's act. She knew all of his secrets. Houdini, in a note found after his death, described her as 'the only one who has actually helped me in my work'. She was a very dutiful and faithful wife, who was extremely supportive of her husband's various exploits.

Upon his arrival in Melbourne, the press immediately interviewed Houdini. *The Argus*, a local Melbourne paper, printed an interview the next day. In many ways this interview echoed the one given to *The Advertiser* a couple of days before. The article was titled 'An Expert In Escapes'. It therefore immediately established Houdini as an escape act rather than a magic act. Houdini reinforced this impression by stating, 'If I might be allowed to coin a word, I would call myself an escapologist.' Thus Houdini established the idea in the public mind that his feats were based on skill.

Much like his interview in Adelaide, Houdini distanced himself from the handcuff business by saying, 'Don't talk to me about handcuffs. I'm through with them.' Despite this, he did recount several of his favourite handcuff stories. Including one where he escaped from handcuffs by threading his shoelace through them and pulling the lock open. He asserted that his was the first handcuff act ever done. A concern with being original preoccupied Houdini throughout the tour. He may have known that 'Hanco', the handcuff king, was performing in Sydney at the same time as he performed in Melbourne.

Houdini also refused the description of magician, saying that 'Magicians are too common.' Here the escapologist once again attempted to distinguish himself from other acts.

Harry Houdini and Bess with entourage would have settled into their hotel suite on Sunday 6 February with anticipation, an anticipation that was shared by the Melbourne public. Houdini's ability to fulfil these high expectations and satisfy the anticipation was about to be tested.

The first performance in Melbourne

Generally, theatre at the time of Houdini's visit could be divided into legitimate and popular forms. The legitimate theatre was characterised by the fact that it was patronised by the upper or upper middle classes. Popular theatre tended to be patronised by the working classes or lower orders. In Australia, more so than in countries like the United States and England, there was a greater crossover between the two. People from all walks of life would visit the vaudeville venues such as the New Opera House and they would also visit the opera, ballet or drama. It was a time of flux in terms of social mobility and social acceptability.

In order to meet and encourage the broadening demand for entertainment, vaudeville and variety theatre owners had attempted to make their form of entertainment less risqué and more family-friendly. The theatres in 1910 were more formal places than they had been forty or fifty years before. The audiences were encouraged to show their appreciation by cheering or clapping rather than throwing objects on stage. It was a time when manners and politeness mattered, and the whole of society was undergoing major technological, cultural and social changes. Houdini was fully ensconced in this age. He was a man of formal manners, a man who projected himself as a respectable married gentleman. His act was firmly associated with the popular brand of entertainment.

At the time of Houdini's appearance in Melbourne, there was a great deal of competition in the entertainment industry. As far as legitimate theatre was concerned, the main competition was the drama. In addition, a new medium, the moving picture, was encroaching upon the theatre's stranglehold. All these avenues were potential competitors with Houdini. It was necessary for him to distinguish himself from them in order to be successful. He had already begun this task with his interviews.

Houdini opened at the New Opera House in Melbourne on Monday evening, 7 February 1910. He was part of a long program of songs, dances and comedy sketches, which began around 8 p.m. and lasted for almost two hours. The Opera House program was under the direction of musical director Fred Hall, stage manager James Bell and business manager Frederic Aydon, who was the brother-in-law of Harry Rickards.

The New Opera House programs of the time consisted of two parts. The first was a series of individual turns by regular Opera House performers such as Fred Bluett, Clyde Cook or George Sorlie. These turns were presented in a minstrel style. The regulars would sit in a semicircle; there would be end men and an interlocutor. The interlocutor was master of ceremonies and straight man to the end men. Regulars would present their individual act in turn. Such acts would be serio-comic songs, dances, or comedy skits. Sometimes the first part would be a revue in which the individual turns were linked by a theme. For example, during Houdini's appearance, a theme used for the first part was 'The Fishing Village'.

After an interval, the second part of the program would be presented. This part was presented in a more traditional vaudeville style. It consisted mainly of imported or speciality acts. The Rickards circuit was unusual in that he often had more than one imported act on the bill. Most vaudeville theatres presented only one. Thus the Martine Brothers, comedy acrobats, shared the bill with Houdini in Melbourne and Lily Langtry shared it with him in Sydney. When Houdini appeared at the New Opera House, he was accompanied by acts such as Fred Curran, the quaint comedian, and Teddie, Decima and Roy McClean. Houdini was scheduled to appear in the second half of the program, second from last, a prime headlining spot.

When the time came, Houdini's appearance on stage was introduced by moving pictures. The first film showed scenes from an escape in 1906. The location was Philadelphia. In the footage, Houdini was shackled and handcuffed by members of the local police force. He then stood upon the Market Bridge and dived into the river below. The film then focused on a group of boatman on the river. They were resting on their oars waiting for Houdini to emerge from the water. After a few minutes, Houdini's head popped above the water line. He was smiling and holding the shackles triumphantly high above his head. He then swam to the nearest boat, was dragged aboard and taken to the wharf. The second piece of film showed a similar scene that had been filmed in April 1909. Houdini was shown leaping into the Seine River from the Paris morgue. It was a suitably macabre location. Houdini's use of moving pictures was an acknowledgement of the power of the new medium. These films also introduced the concept of the manacled bridge-dive to the audience and previewed his own dive from the Queens Bridge into Melbourne's Yarra River.

The films prepared the audience for the appearance of Houdini in the flesh. After they had flickered into darkness, Houdini appeared on stage. He was dressed in black and white evening clothes. A relatively small man, of stocky build, with curly dark hair and a hypnotic gaze. He probably bowed briefly as the audience applauded in recognition.

Houdini gestured and uniformed attendants wheeled a veiled cabinet to the centre of the stage.

A committee of twenty men came from the audience, walked up some stairs and joined Houdini on stage. Members of this committee bound Houdini's hands tightly behind his back. Houdini was still wearing his suit coat as they did so. The escapologist then walked into the curtained cabinet and in seconds the coat was thrown out in front of it. The mystifier then re-emerged. His hands were still securely fastened behind his back.

The next feat was Metamorphosis, or the trunk substitution feat. Houdini's uniformed assistants rolled a large trunk to the front of the stage. Members of the audience committee again secured Houdini's hands behind his back. After ensuring that he was tightly bound, they helped the escapologist climb into a sack. The committee tied and secured the top of the sack over his head. The sack, with Houdini enclosed, was then put into the trunk. The trunk in its turn was roped and nailed shut by the committee. The trunk, accompanied by Bess Houdini, who was dressed in black knickerbockers, was hidden behind a curtain. In a few seconds, Houdini clapped his hands. He popped out from behind the curtain, and appeared in front of the audience. The trunk was wheeled out and opened. The sack was untied and from it emerged Bess Houdini. She was wearing the coat that Houdini had been wearing when he entered the trunk. The fastenings of both trunk and sack looked completely untouched. Bess and Harry had been performing Metamorphosis for many years before they took it to Australia. It was an old trick, but still had great impact on audiences.

For the finale, Houdini escaped from a straitjacket. Clad in a white shirt and black trousers, he was trussed tightly by members of the committee. A contemporary report described the ensuing struggle in graphic terms:

> For the next minute or so, the audience caught fleeting glimpses of a wriggling bundle of white shirt and dress clothes as it bounced and kicked itself about the stage.

In a minute and a quarter the white shirt 'rather kicked about but a good one still' straightened into shape and the audience found itself gazing at a gasping Houdini.

The straitjacket escape was very physically demanding. Houdini later stated that it was performed entirely by muscular exertion.

The audience on the first night was enthusiastic and screamed for more. Houdini bowed and announced that he intended to jump, shackled, into the Yarra River, after he had obtained permission from the authorities.

Newspaper reactions to Houdini's act were mostly positive. *The Age* newspaper described Houdini's feats as 'clever'. It added that the box feat, Metamorphosis, was bewildering and mystifying audiences. It also compared Houdini to Bill Sykes in his knowledge of escaping from police 'furniture'. It added that he was 'a decidedly original performer'. This description must have warmed Harry's heart and would lead to the press using a variety of metaphors in an attempt to classify Houdini's act, the first being the Dickensian references in *The Age*.

The reporter for *The Age* also enthused about the straitjacket escape. The report stated that 'Houdini was tied so tightly, that nothing more than a sigh could escape.' It described the movements he used to escape the jacket as similar to those of a slithering eel, adding that 'outside a moving picture film the thing seemed hardly possible'.

The Opera House advertisement which appeared in the newspapers the day after Houdini's debut described him as presenting the 'most astounding and mystifying entertainment ever seen in the southern hemisphere'. It continued by stating that Houdini was 'recalled and recalled repeatedly greeted and cheered to the echo again'. The advertisement echoed *The Age's* description of an 'Oliver'-like audience screaming for more. Combined, the two descriptions created a picture of unbridled enthusiasm. Houdini mania had captured Melbourne. Rickards and Houdini must have been overjoyed by the reaction.

As Houdini's performances continued to great acclaim over the next week, there was one minor hiccup. This incident was reported in several papers. The press seemed to take Houdini's side in the matter.

The committee man

Although the attitude of the press was positive towards Houdini, the attitude of certain members of the public could be sceptical. This attitude was demonstrated vividly during a Houdini performance on 12 February. The theatre that night was crowded. It was Saturday night and the spectators were celebrating the weekend. Houdini, as was customary, invited a committee of audience members onto the stage. Usually the committee consisted of twenty men, and Houdini knew some of them. One, who may have been a random selection, seemed to have some scepticism about the escapologist's act. He came to the stage and, once there, he approached Houdini and began to search him. He searched the escapologist's pockets and during the search he found a key. The committee man acted as if he had made a great discovery. Houdini attempted to explain that there were no handcuff escapes that night. Thus the key was of no use to him in the performance. The escapologist explained that it was actually the key for his dressing room (or dressing case). The two men began to argue. Houdini asked the man to return the key. The committee man refused. In retaliation Houdini took the man's watch and chain. Unfortunately the chain broke. Houdini asked the man how he enjoyed being deprived of his possessions. Another argument began about who would pay for the broken chain.

Eventually, Mr Aydon, the manager of the theatre, was called to the stage to mediate. The watch and chain were passed to him. The committee man was allowed to keep Houdini's key. The whole incident, including the various arguments, occurred in front of a packed house. The audience was unsure whether this incident was part of the act or a genuine altercation. The newspapers asserted that it was genuine. Houdini later expressed some annoyance with this gentleman's attitude. The papers seemed to agree that the gentleman was spoiling the show. *The Argus* described the man as 'ultra sceptical', whilst *The Age* described him as 'over zealous'.

There are two interesting points to note about this incident. Firstly, the press seemed to believe Houdini when he stated that the key had nothing to do with his act. Indeed, there were no handcuff escapes scheduled for that evening. However, there was a possibility that Houdini could have used the key as a tool in another escape. The press did not mention this possibility. Perhaps they did not want to spoil a good story, or perhaps, in those more polite times, it was common to believe what was said.

The second point was Houdini's reaction to this incident. Surely Houdini had faced sceptics of all kinds before? The picture of Harry Houdini, world-famous escapologist, arguing with an anonymous Australian in front of a full house is not very edifying. In fact, it seemed rather bizarre. Houdini seemed unable to cope with criticism even if it was ridiculous

On the other hand, perhaps it was a publicity stunt. Houdini had a habit of planning these sorts of 'gags', as he called them. He often wrote notes planning them. In one, there was a suggestion that a man and woman should be planted in the audience arguing about whether the man should act as a member of the audience committee. The plan was that as the man rose to his feet to approach the stage, the woman would pull him back. She would nag and eventually leave the theatre. The whole scenario was a scripted bit of nonsense by Houdini to gain a laugh from the crowd. The committee man incident in Melbourne could have been one of these Houdini 'gags'.

Like many incidents that occurred during the Houdini tour, it is difficult to make a definitive judgement in this matter. Where Houdini was concerned, nothing was as it appeared. The broken watch chain and the argument about payment suggested that this was a legitimate confrontation. Houdini could be petty at times and this could have been one of those occasions. Whatever the case, it certainly gained Houdini some publicity from the newspapers.

The Yarra dive

As demonstrated by the movies he had shown to the audience, Houdini had dived, shackled into rivers all around the world. He had told the first-night audience that he planned to perform a similar leap into the Yarra River. He added that this escape would depend on gaining permission from local authorities. That permission was quickly granted and, on Wednesday 16 February, the following advertisement appeared in the papers:

Daring Dive
Houdini, the world famous escapologist will appear at
THE QUEENS BRIDGE
Tomorrow (Thursday) afternoon February 17 at 1.30pm prompt.

Houdini intended to dive into the Yarra, padlocked and chained, and escape from the bonds. The advertisements made it clear that the combined weight of the chains and irons at twenty-five pounds (11.34 kilograms) would carry him to the bottom of the river, where he would have to free himself in order to avoid drowning.

Melbourne at that time was suffering from a heatwave. Tuesday of that week had been hot, Wednesday was even warmer. On that day, the temperature had reached 101 degrees Fahrenheit (38.33 degrees Celsius). Another hot day dawned on Thursday.

That day around 12.30 p.m., people started gathering around the Queens Bridge and surrounding area. *The Age* newspaper described them as 'stevedores, carriers, men of all trades and callings. along with city clerks and office boys'. Pictures taken at the time showed large crowds, mostly men, gathering around the bridge and lining both banks of the river. The more prosperous wore straw-boater hats, dark coats, light shirts and ties. Others wore the uniform of the working man, peaked caps, with white shirts rolled to the elbows. There were men in bowler hats, young and old men with pipes hanging from their mouths. There were women too, with hats and veils shielding their faces from the sun. Many of the spectators sat in wooden rowboats on the river, leaning on the oars waiting for Houdini to arrive. His appeal crossed class and gender boundaries and nowhere was this more evident than in the crowds which appeared to see him that day. There were almost twenty thousand people gathered when 1.30 p.m. approached.

Houdini, the handcuff king and world-famous escapologist, arrived shortly before that time. He was driven to the bridge from the theatre, probably by chauffeur John Jordon. It was a short trip. The car would have dodged trams, horses, buggies, the occasional car, and hordes of people scurrying towards the river. Houdini was accompanied by Frederick Aydon, and his 'German attendant', probably Franz Kukol.

When he left the car, he was clad in a tight-fitting blue bathing costume. It covered him from neck to knee. Houdini leapt up to the parapet of the bridge and held out his hands for the handcuffs. According to *The Age* he acted as if the proceedings were a huge joke and admitted it was a trick.

Kukol passed a heavy chain around his neck and padlocked it underneath his chin. Another chain and padlock were draped around his neck, joined to the original. Regulation handcuffs were snapped to his wrists. The descriptions of the exact bonds differed, but gave the general impression that he was chained from waist to neck. His arms were completely immobilised. Some of the bystanders were invited to test the locks and chains. They pronounced them secure.

Houdini was twenty feet (6.10 metres) above the water, which at low tide was ten feet eight inches (3.25 metres) deep. Taking a deep breath, he dived straight, 'taking a beautiful header, cutting the water clean'.

The crowds craned their necks over the water, anxious to see the escape. They could see nothing. Houdini was covered by the muddy water, which essentially acted as the curtain did in his act. It obscured the escape from prying eyes. Houdini later stated that he was up to his armpits in mud, which, whilst good for obfuscation, complicated the escape.

While the crowd waited for what seemed an eternity for Houdini to reappear, a strange incident occurred.

A man dressed in black approached one of Houdini's assistants. 'Excuse me,' he said, 'are you connected with the chap who has just gone down?'

'Yes,' replied the attendant.

The stranger in black pressed a card into the hand of Houdini's assistant. 'In case he shouldn't come up,' he said.

The assistant later read the card and discovered that it bore the name of a local undertaker. It seemed everybody had recognised the death-defying nature of the feat.

A man leaning over the parapet, with a stopwatch in his hand, timed a couple of minutes, and still Houdini did not appear. The police in their rowboats nervously fingered their corpse grappling irons 'in anticipation of the coroners inquiry'. They circled the river, anxiously watching for signs of the escapologist.

Another few seconds passed and then the wavy-haired head of Houdini poked its way through the water. He was holding the chains in one hand, and smiling. He casually swam breaststroke to a waiting wooden police boat. The police in their white round helmets and blue uniforms pulled him over the side and into the boat.

Houdini stood as they rowed him to shore. He dramatically pointed his finger towards the wharf, looking like an explorer who had just discovered paradise and was planning a landing there. The crowd screamed and cheered at the showman and waved their hats in appreciation. Houdini finally stepped ashore probably acknowledged the cheers either by a bow or wave and was quickly taken back to the Opera House to prepare for that night's show.

The dive was a demonstration of Houdini's remarkable ability to advertise. It had all the features of a carefully organised marketing campaign and many features of a theatrical performance. In fact, its format echoed many of Houdini's stage escapes. The introduction of the lone figure standing chained above the crowd echoed the appearance of the showman on stage. The dramatic and tense wait as he disappeared into the muddy waters recalled Houdini's disappearance behind the curtain during Metamorphosis, and finally the relief of tension as the sole figure emerged safe and well was similar to that felt after he had successfully completed a challenge. Houdini's final dramatic stance on board the boat added to the sense of occasion and theatricality. The feat appealed to the sporting instincts of the throng, and was conducted with all the flair and showmanship that Houdini had honed through years of performance.

The milk can escape

On 26 February 1910, *The Argus* newspaper carried an advertisement for Houdini's new act at the Opera House. The advertisement promised a 'death defying mystery'. It was the first indication that Houdini intended to perform the celebrated milk can escape in Australia.

The advertisement placed emphasis on two important aspects of the feat. Firstly that it was Houdini's own and original invention and secondly that 'failure to release himself means drowning'. Thus did Houdini use a combination of originality and ghoulishness to appeal to his audience.

The milk can escape had its Australian premiere on Saturday 26 February. It replaced Metamorphosis. It was thus presented between the simple coat escape and the straitjacket escape. The milk can escape was regarded as a more exciting feat than Metamorphosis, probably because of the risk it involved.

The presentation of the trick was carefully planned to enhance the aura of risk. It began with Houdini's two uniformed attendants rolling the milk can onto the stage. The usual audience committee was invited to examine the can. It was then filled to the brim with twenty-two pails of water. While it was being filled, Houdini left the stage. He changed from his customary evening clothes and re-entered the auditorium wearing his famous blue swimming costume.

After the can was filled under the sharp eyes of the committee, Houdini addressed the audience. Looking down upon the seated crowd, he gave a short but pertinent speech. He informed them in his slightly accented tones that he was about to risk his life by attempting a very dangerous feat. He then gave a short demonstration of the dangers involved. Houdini asked the audience to attempt to hold their breath as long as he did under water. He then approached the milk can. Stepping into it, he submerged beneath the water without the lid being fastened. He remained in this position for about a minute and a half in full view of the assembled spectators. The fact that few of the audience could match him and hold their breaths for one and a half minutes further enhanced the effect of the trick. This built the tension, heightened the sense of risk and established the necessary mechanics for the feat.

Having established the dangers, it was time for the escape to be performed. There was probably a dramatic drum roll. The audience watched, hushed, as Houdini dramatically re-entered the can. The audience committee gathered around it, and the lid was put in place. It was secured tightly with six spring-loaded padlocks. The committee re-inspected the can and tested the locks. It was then wheeled behind a curtain.

A uniformed attendant, usually Franz Kukol, stood to the side of the stage, holding a large axe in his hand. Houdini had explained that Franz was stationed in this position so that he could smash the can and free Houdini if something went wrong. Franz's presence highlighted the dangerous nature of the escape.

The band played and the audience waited. The man with the axe fingered it nervously. One minute passed and the audience got restless. Two minutes passed and they made further noise. More time passed and panic crept in. Just as the attendant with the axe made a move towards the screen, Houdini reappeared. A huge sigh of relief escaped from the audience. Houdini bowed, looking 'none the worse for his immersion'.

Charles Waller, an Australian magician who witnessed the escape, described it as 'the best thing I saw him do here'. Waller stated that it was briefly done, but Houdini's showmanship was such that it seemed 'marvellous and sensational'.

The Age called the milk can escape 'sensational', and the audience 'loudly cheered' the feat. It was a very mysterious and unusual act.

Some people, however, were convinced that they knew how it was done. On Wednesday 9 March a challenge to Houdini appeared in the papers. It was titled 'Houdini defied'. It read in part,

> Having witnessed your performance of the can mystery, we believe that the main secret is your ability to see through water.

Signed by the Willsmere Certified Milk Company of Bourke Street, Melbourne, it challenged Houdini to escape from the can when it was filled with milk. Houdini accepted the challenge and prepared to deal with it that night.

The challenge specified that employees of Willsmere would fill the can with milk. It added that Houdini attempted the escape at his own risk. Thus it contained the necessary death-defying aspect that Houdini exploited to gain an audience.

That night, Houdini prepared to take the challenge. Dressed in his usual evening clothes, he gave a speech. He emphasised the high-risk nature of the feat he was about to perform. Before attempting the challenge, he stationed an assistant with an axe and a stopwatch near the can. He stated that this was to ensure that if he did not escape the can in a certain amount of time, his life could be saved.

Willsmere provided the milk and filled the can with it. Houdini stepped into it and stayed under for a minute and a half without the lid. Then it was time for the challenge. The employees refilled the can. Houdini stepped in and under the liquid. The lid of the can was placed on top and it was locked with six padlocks. The whole apparatus was curtained off from the audience and they waited.

In less than three minutes, Houdini was free. The can looked undisturbed and was still full of milk, The employees of Willsmere, who had been positive that they had found the escapologist's secret, were stunned. The audience loudly applauded. Houdini just for fun jumped into the milk can again. He came out smiling and dripping with milk.

Later he admitted that it was all a trick, and added with a grin, 'But you don't know how it's done.' The milk was poured away to reassure the public that it would not be reused.

So if the transparency of the liquid did not affect the escape, what was the secret? It was undoubtedly a dangerous escape. The person within the can was crouched low in almost a foetal position for the time that they were submerged. Not only was this uncomfortable, it also made breathing difficult. It was an escape that relied upon Houdini's athletic prowess and his mechanical ingenuity. Houdini had trained himself for it by staying under water in his bathtub at home. He had run long distances to strengthen his lungs and had practised swimming underwater for long periods of time. Houdini's preparation for all his feats was impeccable. He trained his body so that he could perform feats that seemed impossible to the ordinary person.

The secret of the milk can escape was a combination of Houdini's superb physical conditioning and the construction of the can. It had been made specifically for Houdini and he eventually patented the design. The top of the can was doubled, and attached to the rest by two fake rivets. Houdini could hop inside the can when it was full, remove these rivets and remove the top of the can without disturbing the padlocks or the contents. The whole contraption was constructed so that the can could be examined and not reveal its secret. To the outsider it looked like an ordinary, solid, galvanised, iron milk can. It was an ingenious device.

The challenge from Willsmere was one of many challenges that Houdini faced in Melbourne.

The Melbourne challenges

Wherever Houdini travelled, he was challenged, either by the cynical, those desirous of fame, or the insane. While in Melbourne, Houdini was challenged to escape from boxes, glass cases and some impossible situations.

Many of these challenges were bizarre. One asked him to put a loaded gun to his mouth, pull the trigger and escape the consequences, in full view of the audience. Another asked him to escape a coffin filled with quicklime. Yet another, from a lady, was so indelicate that Charles Waller, who later wrote about the Houdini tour, refused to give details.

Houdini accepted many challenges while in Melbourne, far more than he did in Sydney. The challenges in many ways drew upon an older, more interactive element of theatre tradition. Houdini used this tradition and memories of it to increase his audience. He also drew upon his own experience of beer halls and music halls in order to attract attention through the challenges. Strangely this older tradition was combined with a modern marketing method to produce a successful act.

Within the first week of Houdini's engagement, he received his first challenge. Dated 8 February 1910, it was from a group of carpenters and joiners, John Shearer, Zenas Law, Christian Thomsen, and John A. Hunter of Andrew Kerr Pty Ltd, Franklin Street, Melbourne. These gentlemen challenged Houdini to escape from a specially constructed packing case made from timber. They proposed to nail, screw and rope Houdini into the case. They were sure that this would make it 'impossible for you to make your escape'. They were prepared to allow the escapologist to make the attempt in private and also to let him examine the case beforehand. They insisted that he was not to destroy the case while escaping. In addition, they wanted to be permitted to renail the chest immediately before the escape, to prevent Houdini making any preparations. Houdini accepted the challenge and it was set to take place on Friday 11 February.

That night, a large audience gathered to watch Houdini's attempt. He was dressed in his usual evening clothes. He stepped into the packing case and the carpenters and joiners nailed him in. After that had been completed to everybody's satisfaction, a screen was placed around the box and the audience waited.

Charles Waller, who was almost certainly in the audience for this escape, described what happened as he waited for Houdini to emerge:

> Too well do I remember waiting for more than 20 minutes while Houdini was making his escape from a packing case. During all this time we could do no more than watch each other's beards grow and listen to the brassy clangour of an old fashioned music hall band.

According to *The Argus*, the band played popular tunes and the audience sang as they waited. After six minutes they heard a creak. After fifteen minutes, another sound of timber scraping against itself. After twenty-five minutes, Houdini flung back the screen. According to Waller, the audience went 'mad with delight'. Houdini – sweating, coatless and sleeveless – had enraptured and baffled the audience. The box looked completely untouched.

Once again, the features of this escape echoed the strategies employed during the dive and the milk can escape. The dramatic presentation caused a tense wait, which was succeeded by a sense of relief when Houdini appeared. In the matter of playing to the audience's emotions, Houdini was an expert.

The Weekly Times pointed out that if there was one weak spot in Houdini's act, it was the 'small amount of the business that the spectator sees'. The paper added that 'one might as well sit at home and read of his feats'. Houdini recognised this weak point and his elaborate presentation sought to overcome it. He was, it seemed, successful. The theatre-going public of Melbourne was entranced and the challenges to Houdini continued arriving at the theatre and newspapers.

Houdini's next challenge came shortly after he dived into the Yarra. Dated 14 February 1910, it came from somebody who the *Argus* may have described as 'ultra sceptical'. W.M. Morgan and Company of 250–256 Swanston Street, Melbourne, challenged Houdini to escape from a padded cell suit. The suit, made of 'coarse canvasboard belting, straps and leather bindings', restrained the wearer from neck to feet. It was, according to the challengers, used only on dangerous criminals or the murderous insane. W.M. Morgan and Company guaranteed that Houdini would not escape. They insisted that he make the attempt in full view of the audience, to prove 'that you have no traps in the stage or concealed confederates'. Houdini accepted the challenge for Friday 18 February.

Houdini later confided to a Sydney newspaper that he could dislocate his shoulders at will. This undoubtedly aided his escape from such bindings as those constructed by W.M. Morgan.

On the evening of Friday 18 February, three employees of W.M. Morgan and Co. secured Houdini in the suit. They used 'some vigour' in securing him. The sleeves of the suit were tied behind Houdini's back, and his lower limbs were fastened with broad leather bands. The employees had spent fifteen hours constructing the restraint and were confident of success. After securely binding Houdini, they stood back and waited. The stage fortunately was carpeted and Houdini wriggled on the carpet until he managed to free his arms. He then uncrossed them and undid the buckles that bound him. According to *The Weekly Times*, it took Houdini about two minutes to escape from the suit. The newspaper added a light-hearted comment:

> What a blessing it is that Mr Rickards is able to assure us that Houdini is not an insane murderer.

It also stated that, while escaping the suit, Houdini kept up a 'running fire of merry banter'. His successful escape was greeted with loud applause.

Houdini's unusual acrobatic and physical skills allowed him to escape these sorts of bindings easily. It was obvious that he could pick and choose which challenges to attempt and which to refuse. He did in fact refuse at least one challenge and presumably others. Noticeably he preferred feats such as the one above, which involved acrobatic skill. With the ability to dislocate his shoulders, he could perform these escapes in front of an audience.

Each escape, however, was physically demanding and exhausting. Houdini was performing them at least once a week. He would usually drop the rest of the performance when doing a challenge, yet it was still a very physically punishing schedule.

On 21 February, Houdini received his next weekly challenge. It was from saddlery workers A.J. Chant and L.H. Elburn. Messrs Chant and Elburn wished to bind Houdini to a workbench or table,

> His head being held down by a broad leather collar encircling his neck, his arms drawn crosswise his hands strapped to the edges of a table, halter straps and thick leather belt fastening down his body and four special straps made in manacle style securing his ankles.

They added that all straps would be out of Houdini's reach. They also made it clear that they did not want interference from the Opera House staff and that Houdini was to perform the feat in full view of the audience. Houdini added a condition himself. The leather collar for securing his neck must not be drawn so tightly as to strangle him. Houdini was willing to do almost anything to publicise his act. Throttling himself, however, was not one of those things.

Messrs Chant and Elburn wagered £5 that Houdini would not escape their prison. They were self-described working men and could not afford to wager more. Unfortunately the two men, employees of Shakespeare and Co. saddlery of 437 Bourke Street, lost their £5. On Friday night, 25 February, Houdini attempted the challenge. He took thirteen minutes to escape the contraption. Before Houdini was imprisoned, one of the committee men drawn from the audience wanted to attempt the feat. Much time was wasted with this task. His escape was unsuccessful whilst Houdini became £5 richer.

The challenges revealed much of the speculation that was gripping those who had seen Houdini's act. The conditions attached to the escapes gave clues to how the audience thought they were done. W.M. Morgan thought Houdini used a trapdoor or a hidden confederate. Messrs Elburn and Chant seemed to think that the accomplice was a theatre employee. Many people were therefore thinking of the act as a trick, but a trick perpetrated by natural means. Houdini encouraged this view by openly stating that escapes such as the milk can mystery were a trick. Noticeably, none of these people seemed to be considering supernatural agency for Houdini's success. On the other hand, the person who challenged Houdini to escape the consequences of a fired revolver probably thought he was accomplishing his escapes through supernatural means.

Houdini's next challenge came from trained nurses and asylum attendants and was dated 28 February. Its publication followed a well established procedure. It first appeared as an advertisement in the newspapers on the Wednesday before the feat was to be attempted.

This advertisement was headed 'Will he escape?' and detailed the challenge in full.

Three men who were associated with Beechworth Hospital, Kew Asylum and Yarra Road Asylum issued this challenge. They wanted to wrap Houdini in sheets and linens, and secure him to a hospital bed. They would then soak him with several buckets of water. The water would cause the linens to shrink, thus binding Houdini tightly. The gentlemen believed that Houdini would soon be happy to ask them for release. Once again, the test was to take place in full view of the audience.

The challenge was placed in the papers up to and including the Friday it was to be performed. This placement was virtually identical for all the challenges. It built suspense for the feat and created public awareness of it.

Houdini agreed to take this particular test on Friday 4 March. *The Age* described it as 'his most severe Melbourne test'.

By this time the press must have been accustomed to Houdini's successes, because his triumphant escape from this challenge was only briefly mentioned. *The Australasian* was in fact sceptical about the value of the challenges. They stated that

> The public challenge to a stage celebrity to do something which everyone feels quite sure that he can do always excites suspicion.

The paper added that the challenges were not necessary, as there was no magic in the performances. The general public, however, disagreed with this assessment and continued to patronise Houdini shows.

On Wednesday 9 March, Houdini successfully escaped from the challenge given by the Willsmere Company. That is, he escaped from a milk can filled with milk. This was the first challenge attempted in that very busy week.

On the Friday of that week, Friday 11 March, he attempted another challenge. Harry Burton, W. Brown, F. Collister and C. James, able-bodied seamen, proposed to truss Houdini in a manner which, should he escape, would be the 'task of your life'. *The Referee* newspaper had stated that many of the challenges could be cruel, and this challenge certainly fell into that category. The challenge was very detailed. Firstly the sailors would place a stick behind Houdini's knees and tie his wrists to it on either side. Secondly they would lash and tie him on his back to a wooden plank. Thirdly they would weave a network of sash cord around him to prevent any knots slipping. Houdini was not permitted to cut any ropes to escape, and was to perform the challenge in front of the audience.

It took the able-bodied seamen fifteen minutes to tie Houdini down. Apparently their method was once used for mutinous crew members and the sailors were very thorough in their knots and ties. Houdini wriggled and twisted and finally after thirty-three minutes gained freedom from the predicament. In the process, he scraped the skin off both wrists. He was completely exhausted by the end of it.

Houdini's vast experience of public challenges made it easy for him to choose those from which he could escape. Most of the Melbourne challenges resembled some he had previously attempted in either the United States or Europe. This control was a method by which he could maintain his image and also manipulate an audience. The similarity of the Sydney challenges to those in Melbourne also suggested a large amount of control behind the scenes. Houdini was a performer who could enthral an audience; he was also a man who was master of his destiny, and a highly intelligent manipulator of his image.

There was one final challenge This was from a group of rope makers. Mr A.C. Downs and Mr F. Madden of Downs and Sons Pty Ltd challenged Houdini to escape after being tied to a chair. The challenge was dated 15 March. The gentlemen proposed tying Houdini with a particular brand of rope called Russian Hemp. It was braided cotton rope, which would not shrink or give. The challenge was set to take place during the show of Friday 18 March. On that same day, Houdini had flown for the first time at Diggers Rest. This aviation feat dominated the newspapers and overshadowed the challenge. Although there was little press coverage, it appeared that he successfully overcame it.

Sceptic

The attitudes of the press and public were almost uniformly positive towards Houdini while he was in Melbourne. There was, however, a minority which was cynical. One of these was known only as 'Sceptic'.

Sceptic wrote an anonymous letter to *The Age* newspaper. The letter was dated 10 March and printed in *The Age* on 11 March. It outlined concerns that Sceptic had with the able-bodied seamen's challenge to Houdini.

The names and addresses of the challengers had been given in the newspaper advertisements. As published in *The Age* they were

Harry Burton, 22 Rosa St, Port Melbourne.
W. Brown, 2 Dover St, Port Melbourne
F. Collister, Oxford St, Port Melbourne
C. James, 189 Dow St, Port Melbourne.

They were all identified as able-bodied seamen.

Sceptic had obviously seen these advertisements. He had used the Melbourne City Directory to check the names and addresses of the challengers. After doing so, Sceptic had found that some of the addresses printed in the advertisements did not exist. For example, there was no 'Oxford Street' in Port Melbourne. In addition, Sceptic pointed out that the names of some of the challengers did not match their stated addresses. In fact, the name F. Collister did not appear in the directory at all. Sceptic thought that these discrepancies reflected suspiciously upon the famed escapologist, Houdini, and concluded in the letter that

> These facts may serve to enhance the interest which these 'challenges' invariably arouse.

Houdini, as was typical, responded to these accusations promptly. He took the same route as Sceptic and wrote to *The Age*. His letter was published on 12 March. In his response, Houdini corrected some of the address information contained in the challenge. He explained the mistakes as being due to poor legibility in the hand-written challenge. Houdini also stated in response to sceptic's letter that

> Were the letter written in a friendly and upright manner after due investigation, I would doff my hat to 'Sceptic'.

The idea that Houdini would 'doff his hat' to Sceptic seemed strange. Was it an admission of some chicanery afoot, or was it merely recognition of Sceptic's investigative skills? Houdini, who obviously resented the tone of Sceptic's letter added that

> The sneering manner and the innuendo shows the spirit in which 'Sceptic' parades himself.

Houdini, after correcting the address information, then concluded his reply with a sneering remark of his own:

> And in looking over that worthy and much consulted book, the Melbourne City directory I also fail to find the name and address of anyone named 'Sceptic.'

The Age newspaper printed both letters in full and reviewed the challenge that had concerned Sceptic. Taking Houdini's side on the issue, the newspaper stated that he had met the challenge and beat the sailors 'fairly and squarely, and there could be no doubt whatever concerning the genuineness of his feat'.

Charles Waller, who knew Houdini personally throughout the Australian tour, thought that Houdini could be a petty man. He stated that

> He could be petty enough, and quarrelsome enough too, with those who opposed him or who were not entirely for Houdini.

First flight

One reason for Houdini's trip to Australia was his desire to be an aviation pioneer. Houdini was attempting to become the first person to fly a powered aircraft in Australia. His attempts to fulfil this quest involved a great deal of danger. The vehicle he was attempting to fly was obsolete. He was not a very experienced pilot. There was also a lack of facilities such as storage space, suitable venues, and mechanical expertise available to him in Australia. Houdini had to carry his own spare parts and import his own mechanic, Monsieur Brassac, from Europe to service his Voisin biplane.

In terms of aviation in 1910, the Voisin was an older machine. Gabriel Voisin had designed it in 1905. The Voisin represented a European view of flying at that time, basically that planes were a kind of flying car to be dragged through the air, the pilot's role being to drive it or drag it along. This idea was antithetical to the Wright brothers, who saw the pilot as being an integral part of the machine. The Wright brothers' success was a testament to the efficacy of their thinking.

The Voisin was cumbersome, and also had no control for roll. This lack of control meant that the machine could not fly safely in windy conditions. The problem of wind plagued Houdini throughout his Australian aviation trials. One advantage the Voisin had over the Wright aircraft was that it was easier to become a proficient pilot of the Voisin. The Wright planes required the pilot to play a more active role. Thus it took longer to learn how to fly them.

The plane arrived in Melbourne on 22 February 1910 and was set up in a tent at Diggers Rest. In 1910, Diggers Rest was primarily a rural spot and Houdini's plane was set up in a paddock called Plumpton's field. The field was fenced and dotted around the edges with eucalyptus trees. It was also being used for its intended purpose as grazing land when Houdini was conducting his aviation experiments.

Houdini's avowed aim was to become the first man to make a controlled powered flight in Australia. He did, however, have competitors. Fred Custance and F.H. Jones in South Australia were making attempts at flight with a monoplane at the same time as Houdini. Mr Ralph Banks was also attempting to fly at Diggers Rest in a Wright brothers' aircraft.

On 18 March 1910, *The Age* reported that Mr F.C. Custance had created several records in South Australia the previous day by flying a monoplane. He apparently covered three miles (4.8 kilometres) in just over five minutes at a height of twelve to fifteen feet (3.6 to 4.5 metres). *The Age* added that Mr Custance had crashed upon landing. On 26 March, *The Australasian* newspaper was also reporting the Custance flight. This report was more detailed. It described Custance as a 'motorist' and stated that his first flight had successfully landed. It also stated that the second attempt had resulted in a crash that had damaged the plane, although the pilot had escaped harm. *The Australasian* stated that this was the first flight in Australia and that it had occurred in a Bleriot monoplane. Ralph Banks also reportedly made several successful short flights before Houdini's trials.

On 19 March 1910, *The Age* and *The Argus* were reporting Houdini's successful flights. These flights were witnessed, photographed, filmed and attested to in writing. They were then, and are generally now, regarded as the first successful controlled powered flights on Australian soil.

For some weeks, Houdini had been driving out to Diggers Rest to experiment with the Voisin plane. He had been leaving Melbourne early in the morning and travelling the twenty miles (32.19 kilometres) to Diggers Rest before sunrise. The constant commute, in addition to his physically demanding performance schedule, was exhausting the escapologist.

On the day of his historic flights, Houdini arrived at Diggers Rest around 5 a.m. The trials began at 8 a.m. on 18 March 1910. Monsieur Brassac, after making some final adjustments to the plane, muttered 'Un, deux, trois' and twisted the propeller. The plane sped along the track at thirty miles per hour (38.28 kilometres per hour) and after forty or fifty yards (thirty-six to forty-six metres) rose into the air. The great machine, with HOUDINI emblazoned on its tail, was airborne for less than a minute. The landing was smooth.

On his second flight that day, Houdini covered between one and two miles (1.6 to 3.2 kilometres). There was a problem with the landing, however. The plane ran along the ground with its nose dragging, and its tail in the air. Houdini was preparing to jump to safety, but quickly righted the craft. His assistants were quick to gather around and help him.

The third flight was the most successful. It lasted about three and a half minutes. Houdini circled for about two miles (3.2 kilometres) at an altitude estimated as up to one hundred feet (30.48 metres). As he saw a pile of rocks beneath him, Houdini later described himself as thinking,

> Gee…here's trouble, and I sent her up a bit then I laughed at myself and started to come down.

The witnesses that day included Houdini's assistants and aviation competitors. All signed a document attesting to what they saw:

> We the undersigned, do hereby testify to the fact that on the above date, about 8 o'clock am, we witnessed Harry Houdini in a Voisin Biplane (a French heavier than air machine), make three successful flights of from 1min to 3.1/2min, the last flight being of the last mentioned duration. In his various flights he reached an altitude of 100ft, and in his longest flight traversed a distance of more than two miles.

(signed)
Harold J. Jagelman, Kogarah NSW
Robert Howie, Diggers' Rest
A. Brassac, Paris
Walter P. Smith, 4 Blackwood Street, North Melbourne
F. Enfield Smithells, care of Union Bank, Melbourne
Ralph C. Banks, Melbourne motor garage
Franz Kukol, Vienna
H.L. Vickery, Highgate, England
John H. Jordan, 11 Francis Street, Ascotvale.

Banks, Smithells, Jagelman and Smith were Houdini's competitors, and were working together on Ralph Banks's Wright aircraft. Mr Banks had crashed on 1st March, destroying his plane. Franz Kukol and Vickery were Houdini's stage assistants and John Jordon was his chauffeur. The fact that Houdini's competitors signed a document

35

testifying to his successful flights was an indication of a more civilised age. These gentlemen could applaud the feats of their rivals without rancour.

When driving back to Melbourne that day, Houdini enthused to a reporter about his new hobby:

> As soon as I was up all my muscles relaxed and I sat back feeling a sense of ease. Freedom and exhilaration, that's what it is.

Houdini, the man who sought freedom from the bonds of handcuffs, straitjackets and gaol cells, was now seeking it in a more dangerous medium, the air.

Houdini regarded the flights on 18 March as the first successful flights in Australia. From that time he tended to sign photographs of himself with the appellation 'The first successful aviator in Australia' or something similar. It was as if, by continually repeating the fact, he could make it true. Indeed, this is what happened. For example, in correspondence the State Library of Victoria in 1981 was dating Houdini's first flight as 16 March rather than 18 March. This was a date that Houdini often used and which made his flight before that of Custance. It was a neat bit of historical rewriting. The plaque that Houdini was given in 1910 to commemorate the flight also had this date.

On Saturday 19 March, Houdini attempted another flight, However, winds kept him to only one attempt of twenty-nine seconds. By the time Sunday 20 March arrived, news of Houdini's flights had spread. People were beginning to gather at Plumpton's field. Cars began to roll up, horses and buggies and horse riders arrived and a spring cart brought a band of young men from Melbourne. *The Argus* estimated that approximately one hundred and twenty people gathered to watch the flying. Houdini warned the people to stay beneath the trees. 'I am afraid of trees and you will be safe there.'

Despite this, some of the spectators did not listen to him and one strayed into his line of flight on horseback. This put both pilot and rider in danger and the paper was keen to point this out. Flying etiquette was becoming a part of the daily news.

Houdini's first flight on this day lasted for less than a minute. His second was far more spectacular. He quickly rose to a height of about forty feet (12.19 metres) and circled the field to loud applause. After completing the first circuit, the plane, possibly because of wind, became momentarily vertical, a dangerous moment that had Brassac muttering, and the more knowledgeable members of the crowd holding their breaths. Houdini righted the plane and circled twice more. Mr A. McCracken timed the flight at three and a half minutes. After this second flight, the weather turned windy and it was thought advisable to discontinue flying.

There were further flights at Diggers Rest, including a flight on Monday 21 March. On that day, Houdini left Melbourne at 4.05 a.m. and, driven by Jordon, made his way to Diggers Rest. His car was followed by one containing Mr John Dixon and a party of yachtsmen from Sydney.

As they drove to Plumpton's field, Houdini's car narrowly escaped an accident with a wagon. The driver of the wagon was apparently asleep. Houdini, ever superstitious, commented that the narrow escape 'means good luck for me today'. The two cars arrived at Digger's Rest around 5 a.m. It had taken them almost an hour to travel the twenty miles (32.19 kilometres). The occupants of the cars noted that there was a group of about thirty people present.

Three flights were made that day. Mr Walter Marks of Sydney and an *Argus* reporter timed them. The first flight occurred just before 7 a.m.; it lasted for approximately one minute and was not spectacular. The second flight was more successful. At almost exactly 7 a.m., Houdini took the Voisin to the air. It completed several circles. Its altitude whilst aloft varied widely; at one moment it would be a hundred feet (30.48 metres) high and then would drop to about twenty or thirty feet (six to nine metres). These fluctuations were caused by the variable winds. At one stage, the plane became almost vertical and Houdini was in real danger; he righted the plane in time to avoid disaster. In all, this flight lasted for seven minutes. It was the longest flight recorded in Victoria.

Houdini landed the plane and prepared for a third flight. When he did so, a willy wagtail, a small Australian native bird, hopped on top of the plane and chirped happily at the serious men milling around. Houdini commented on the creature, 'He's telling me I can't fly worth a cuss.'

The third flight on that day lasted one minute thirty-three seconds and reached an altitude of one hundred feet (30.48 metres). Houdini then concluded the flights for the day.

Some of the gathered spectators signed a testament certifying the details of the Houdini's second flight that day. It was issued to the press and read:

Diggers Rest March 21st 1910.

This document certifies that Harry Houdini at 7 o'clock this morning performed the record Australian flight in a Voisin bi-plane , remaining in the air for 7 min 37 secs, in the presence of 30 witnesses including the undersigned. Houdini's movements were plainly hampered by a cross-current of wind which was pronounced by experienced spectators to be distinctly dangerous. He reached a height of from 90 to 100 ft.

(signed)
Walter M. Marks, Solicitor, Sydney, Yacht *Culwulla*
John Dixon, Praban, Yacht Sayorana
D.W. McCay, *The Argus* Reporter, Melbourne
Wal E. Moore, Sydney, Yacht *Culwulla*
A. Bindo Serani, Consul for the Italian Touring Club, Melbourne
F.C. MacKillop, Yacht *Culwulla*
Marc Pourpe, St Kilda, Sydney
Charles H. Elliott, Brighton
James I. Watson, Brighton Beach
Isabel A. Watson, Brighton Beach
Verona Watson, Brighton Beach
F. Enfield Smithells, c/o Union Bank
J.H. Jordon, 11 Francis St, Ascotvale
George J. Hone, Middle Brighton
H.J. Jagelman, Kogarah, Sydney.

Once again amongst the signatories were Houdini's competitors and assistants. Many of these names were those which had signed the testament of 18 March. The men associated with the yacht *Culwulla*, who also signed the document, were fairly prominent. Walter Marks was from a wealthy Sydney family and his father had been a local council member. Walter later became a member of Australia's Federal parliament.

Another man taking an interest in Houdini's flights was Richard Gardner Casey Senior. He was a former member of the Queensland Parliament and chairman of the Victoria Racing Club. Casey was a very wealthy and influential man in 1910. He drove his son, also Richard, and a school friend to Diggers Rest to see Houdini's flights.

Richard junior was almost twenty years old at the time and studying to be an engineer at Melbourne University. In 1969, in one of his last letters as Governor General of Australia, Richard junior recorded his reactions on that day:

> My father and I and a school friend of mine (Randolph Cresswell), son of Admiral Sir William Cresswell, who founded the Australian Navy, drove out to Diggers Rest in one of the early motor cars, where we saw Houdini fly. I was most impressed and excited and talked hard about it all the way back to Melbourne. My friend Randolph Cresswell stood this for some time and then said 'I don't know why you are so worked up about this flight. In a few years time there will be no more romance about this sort of thing than about driving a tram.'

The excited Richard later became a celebrated public figure.

The excitement that the flights generated in Victoria was immense. The combination of Houdini with the mystery and romance of flight left a lasting impression on those who witnessed it. Among those witnesses were the Melbourne elite. Businessmen, future politicians and the children and wives of the wealthy all watched Houdini fly.

There are several photos of Houdini in flight. One photo published in *The Argus* sums up the time. The plane flies crookedly above Plumpton's field, looking as if it has just left the ground. A group of eucalyptus trees are beneath it in silhouette and a few men stand around holding their hats, looking upwards. In the shadow of the plane are two horses, idly grazing on the grass below, ignoring the advancing technology. The picture is a summary of the changes about to occur in everyday life due to the march of industry and technology. It is a neat juxtaposition of the old and new ways.

After his last exploits at Diggers Rest, it was time for Houdini to pack his plane, his entourage, his equipment and himself into a train bound for Sydney. He was due to perform there on Easter Monday.

Houdini's Arrival in Sydney

Houdini, the handcuff king, who had baffled the Western world, arrived in Sydney on Easter Sunday, 27 March 1910. Upon arrival, he gave a brief interview to the press. Houdini told them that he had begun his career as an acrobat. He then proceeded to tell a story of his early years. One of his feats was bending over backwards and picking up a pin with his eye. This was an unusual, difficult and startling feat. He laughed when he related this anecdote. It was the same story he had told the Melbourne press upon his arrival a month before and one of the many theatrical anecdotes that peppered his conversation during the Australian tour.

Houdini then added a short statement where he announced his intention to retire from the stage after the Australian tour in order to pursue aviation. This was the same story he had given to the Melbourne and Adelaide press, but with the new dimension of aviation added. Perhaps he hoped to capitalise upon his new-found aviation fame. It was a statement he repeated often while in Sydney and illustrated the depth of the passion for his new hobby. However, after leaving Australia, Houdini rarely flew. His abandonment of aviation showed an unexpected fickleness in his character. Unexpected because surely, the basis of his fame was a patient, long-endured apprenticeship? The rapidity with which he gave up aviation suggested that Charles Waller may have been right when he stated that Houdini's aviation experiments were more about publicity than history.

Houdini was careful to define himself as an escapologist during this initial interview. He thus continued disassociating himself from the magician label. His definition of himself as an escapologist dealt with claims that his feats were due to supernatural agency. Houdini, by denying the magic label, was emphasising the fact that his performances were due to physical ability.

This interview was so similar to his interview in Melbourne that it is possible that the Sydney press merely copied that interview for their own purposes. Alternatively, perhaps Houdini was repeating his own stories, either through exhaustion or because of the successful reception they had received in Melbourne. It could also have been the result of a well rehearsed line of patter that was designed to promote Houdini's act.

By Monday 28 March 1910, when the interview was published, Houdini had established certain themes and concerns. Two of these were his intention to retire and the fact that he considered himself an escapologist rather than a magician. He had also gained valuable exposure through the newspaper coverage of his arrival. All that was left was for Houdini to follow through on the promises given by The Tivoli Theatre, Harry Rickards and himself. He had to prove himself 'the absolute greatest and most astounding artist (without exception) that had ever appeared in Australia'.

The Sydney Tivoli performance

In order to see Houdini's first performance in Sydney on 28 March, it was necessary to purchase tickets. They could be bought for a price of one shilling or three shillings from either the Tivoli Theatre or Palings. Palings, a store located at 338 George Street, Sydney, near the present Wynard Station, sold pianos, and other musical paraphernalia. It was long a purveyor of such items to the people of Sydney. A booking fee of one shilling was charged if the ticket was bought at the store.

That night, the audience arrived at the theatre in a variety of conveyances. The wealthier drove their genuine De Dion eight to ten horsepower motor cars, with glass windscreen and cape hood, costing £185. The less wealthy could have travelled via Mr Wilkes's horse-driven Yankee staircase omnibus. This vehicle travelled the road from Glebe in inner Sydney to the Tivoli theatre via the Pyrmont Bridge, a route that can still be travelled today. Others could have driven their own horse-pulled sulkies or carriages.

Regardless of mode of transport, the audience, whether in the stalls or circle, were treated to the same performance. Their view was unobstructed. Clutching their free programs that included pictures of Lily Langtry, Houdini, Harry Rickards and his brother, the theatre manager, John C. Leete, the audience would have settled in noisily. It was a first-night audience quivering in anticipation. The program included this request:

> Each lady, who during the performance, removes her hat or ornaments for the hair which obstructs the view of anyone in the audience shows a graceful consideration for the pleasure of others.

Many ladies would have shown this graceful consideration as they settled in their seats. This short notice was an example of how the theatre was attempting to broaden its audience and regulate their behaviour. The variety theatres in particular were attempting with much success to include families and middle-class people amongst their regular patrons; part of this attempt involved formalising the theatre experience.

The audience was treated to a long program that in many respects echoed the program presented in Melbourne. The first part opened with 'Happy Holland', a revue piece with a Dutch theme, complete with windmills, produced by Harry Rickards. Mr Bert Lindsay's comic song 'My wife's gone to the country' continued the first part. Miss Dolly Dormer then performed a 'serio comic song and skipping rope dance'. Mr James Hinchy followed this with the ballad 'My Beloved Queen'. Mr Will White danced to his song 'I love my wife', and Miss May Lewis gave a song and dance, 'Love Me'. Three more soloists followed and the first part of the evening was concluded by the triple song and dance 'Pantomime Sketch' by the Three Mascottes. The grand finale of part one was the famous Tivoli ballerinas.

Overall, the first part consisted of typical Tivoli fare. The regular performers of the Tivoli circuit produced a series of song and dance numbers with comic, amorous or patriotic themes. At this stage the audience was anxiously anticipating the headliners who appeared in the second half of the show. The tension would have increased during the five-minute interval after the ballerinas took their bow.

A managerial announcement was placed after the interval in the printed program. The contents of the announcement were easily understood, and the patrons may have passed part of the five-minute interval reading it:

> Mr Rickards has much pleasure in announcing that he will present, (at each and every performance) to the Sydney public, the absolute greatest and most astounding artist (without exception) that has ever appeared in Australia. The original. The only HOUDINI.

Following interval, the show continued. The Tivoli orchestra, led by Mr Emanuel Aarons, played the march 'Blaze away Glory'. The Two Prices, billed as being from Scotland, then appeared. Mr Ted Kalman, a comic singer, was next. His songs included the nonsensical abbreviation song that included the lines

> Business was slack, so I went to Port Hack
> to spend a few mins by the sea.

The King of Coins, Mr Alan Shaw, followed the comic. He was one of the international headliners of the night. The Bricklayer and the Labourer, singers, were next. Two more soloists followed, and then The Wille Brothers took the stage. They were said to be direct from the London Hippodrome. Their act consisted of pole balancing, and they were accomplished acrobats who were well received by the audience. Miss Olga Grey, an Australian mimic, followed the acrobats, and in turn was followed by Mr Ted Dawson, a comedian. Finally, after the last notes of Mr Dawson's song 'You're the One' faded, it was time for 'The Greatest and Most astounding engagement ever made', Houdini.

The audience had been treated to acrobats, mimics, comedians, singers, and the King of Coins, and was now to be treated to the Original Handcuff King. Houdini's act in Sydney was almost identical to his act in Melbourne. It began with film of his feats in Paris and Philadelphia. After the films, the man himself appeared on stage. He was dressed in evening clothes. *The Daily Telegraph*, a Sydney daily newspaper, described him as 'A short, sturdy man with a broad forehead and keen grey eyes'.

In pictures taken during the stay, he looked intense and severe. He seemed a man serious about his profession. He spoke with an American accent and *The Sydney Morning Herald* commented on his 'laboured enunciation'. He had just turned thirty-six years old when he stepped on the stage of the Tivoli for the first time. The crowd cordially welcomed his appearance.

After acknowledging the applause, a committee of gentlemen joined Houdini on stage. This committee secured his hands behind his back. He then popped behind a curtain and in a trice threw his coat out in front of it. He returned to the front of the stage with his hands still bound. This escape was exactly as the one performed in Melbourne. After this he performed Metamorphosis, where he escaped from a secure trunk, exchanging places with Bess.

Metamorphosis began with the audience committee fastening the escapologist's hands behind him. He was then put into a sack and sealed within it. The sack containing Houdini was put into a trunk. The trunk was closed, roped and locked. Then it was placed behind a curtain, with Bess standing beside it. In a few seconds, Houdini would emerge from behind the curtain. The trunk would be opened and Bess would pop out tied within the sack.

The actual escape, however, began as soon as Houdini was within the trunk. Firstly, Houdini untied his hands. This was an easy feat at that stage of his career. He then took a small cutting implement, which he had secreted on his person, and sliced the bottom of the sack, freeing himself. He was probably already free before the trunk was behind the curtain. The process of tying and padlocking the trunk at this stage distracted the audience. Bess too would have been attracting their attention.

When the trunk was safely behind the curtain, all that was

necessary was for Houdini to press a lever inside it. The side of the trunk folded inward and he escaped without disturbing the ropes and locks. Bess climbed inside both trunk and sack and took his place. When the trunk was reopened, Bess would be freed from the trunk and sack. She would be standing on the hole in the sack, hiding it from view. The whole substitution, given the Houdinis' years of experience, only took seconds.

Houdini's final feat that night was to escape a straitjacket in full view of the audience. This feat was praised by the Sydney newspapers and heartily cheered by the crowd. Houdini concluded his performance by making a speech. He would have been coatless, probably sweating from the exertion of escaping from the straitjacket. A short, breathless man, addressing just over one thousand people.

The speech stated the themes and issues that had concerned Houdini throughout the Australian tour. During it he stated that although many of his feats had been imitated, he was their originator. He added that he intended to retire from performance to take up aviation. This, then, would be his first and last performance in Australia. In relation to this, he stated that his biplane was en route from Victoria and that he intended to fly it in Sydney. This announcement was greeted with cheers. Finally he stated that when his name as the handcuff king had been forgotten, his reputation would be established in Australian history as the first man to fly there in a machine heavier than air. This statement showed that Houdini considered himself to be Australia's first aviator. Custance and other competitors were conveniently forgotten.

Houdini's act was not the end of the program. He was followed by one of the most famous women of the age, Lily Langtry. The Three Mascottes reappeared and Mr George Sorlie, a Tivoli regular, concluded the evening's entertainment. Houdini, however, was the highlight of the evening and his act naturally overshadowed the worthy efforts of the other members of the cast.

On Monday 29 March, reviews of Houdini's performance began appearing in the Sydney press. *The Sydney Morning Herald* described the act in detail. It noted that the use of moving pictures in an act had been used before by Mr Henry Lee. It called Metamorphosis 'wonderful'. The *Herald*'s coverage was restricted to the amusement pages of the paper, and this continued throughout Houdini's Sydney tour. *The Daily Telegraph* review of Houdini, published on 29 March, was more enthusiastic. This review described Houdini's feats as 'mystifying'. It also noted that Metamorphosis was a feat 'with which audiences are familiar'. This implied that it had been performed in Sydney before Houdini's arrival. *The Sydney Mail*, a weekly newspaper, dated 30 March, published a short review of Houdini's act. It described the act as 'noteworthy'. It was not an overly enthusiastic response. This review also stated that some of Houdini's boasts about his escapology feats 'may be a trifle exaggerated'.

In light of this press coverage, Houdini's speech at the conclusion of his performance was significant. His assertion that he was the originator of the feats could have been a response to a cynicism he was detecting in the press. Alternatively, he could have heard of Hanco the handcuff king's performance the previous month. His dislike and distaste for those he termed imitators was repeatedly emphasised when he was in Sydney.

It was typical of Houdini to appeal directly to the audience for validation. He did this on more than one occasion. Houdini tended to confront criticism or negative comment aggressively and directly. His speeches to audiences around the world were often used to justify his actions. They were also used to enhance his reputation.

The speech was also a reflection of Houdini the man. It seemed to show an uncertain side to his character. He was a man who was unsure about his fame and needed to constantly reassert it by claiming originality.

Autumn in Australia

The first week of Houdini's engagement was a great success. He played matinees on Wednesdays and Saturdays and appeared at every evening performance. It was a busy schedule of a physically demanding act.

The Tivoli theatre on 2 April, the second Saturday of his engagement, was crowded. There was standing room only at the evening performance. *The Daily Telegraph* reported that every seat in the stalls and dress circle had been booked before the doors had opened. An attempt to reserve a part of the gallery had been refused by the Tivoli management. Obviously Houdini was proving to be a huge draw. The crowds gathered, attended, were mystified and applauded Houdini for the whole of the next week.

In addition, the press coverage of Houdini became more effusive during the second week of his tour in Sydney. The papers mentioned the straitjacket escape on more than one occasion. They seemed particularly impressed that it occurred in full view of the audience. *The Herald* referred to it as the 'extraordinary struggle with a strait jacket' and described it as 'marvellous'. *The Daily Telegraph* called it 'amazing' and said that the audience had greeted the feat with 'enthusiasm'. The press emphasised the physical aspects of the escape. *The Herald* pointed out the great exertion and violent contortions required to overcome the straitjacket. It described Houdini as an athlete when discussing it. It added that 'the exertion was evidently tremendous'.

The Sydney Mail printed a picture of Houdini about to be secured in the straitjacket. He appeared to be wearing a bow tie and was shown standing impassive as an assistant tied the back fastenings of the jacket. Its sleeves dangled towards the ground, almost reaching the floor. The caption read in part, 'this is one of the many marvellous performances by this remarkable man'.

Theatre Magazine became almost poetic when discussing the straitjacket escape:

> If only all the people in wretchedness and shame-in asylums and prisons-could free themselves from their bonds as Houdini escapes from his straight jacket!

The same article added, 'In olden days he would have been slain by a superstitious populace.' The straitjacket escape caused comment and excited attention from the Sydney press.

Probably in response to this attention, Houdini eventually revealed the secret of the straitjacket escape to a journalist. He stated that he had a round back, and that he could dislocate his shoulders. This gave him some slack when tied in the jacket. He could thus free his hands to undo the back fastenings and subsequently free himself. The fact that Houdini revealed this fact suggested that he was again stressing the athletic aspect of his feats.

On Monday 4 April, Houdini's Voisin aeroplane arrived from Melbourne. The arrival of the plane added one more activity to Houdini's crowded schedule. At this time he began early morning jaunts to Rosehill racecourse, where the plane was stored. It was the continuation of an exhausting schedule that had begun in Melbourne.

On Saturday 9 April, Houdini introduced the milk can escape to his performance. It was advertised as

> His own Invention…as it is impossible to obtain air within the can, failure means death by drowning.

The milk can escape replaced Metamorphosis. The advertising was similar to that in Melbourne. The death-defying nature of the act was emphasised, as was the fact that it was Houdini's invention. It was also performed in the same way as it was performed in Melbourne, complete with curtain, assistant standing to one side with the axe and the tense wait for Houdini to reappear.

The milk can escape involved a great deal of audience participation. Patrons were invited to come onto the stage and inspect the locks and supervise while the can was filled with water. In addition, the advertisements for the escape invited everybody to bring their own locks. An invitation that conjures the image of Edwardian ladies and gentlemen sitting in a plush theatre rattling their locks like Marley's ghost rattled his chains.

The personification of the chained and padlocked spectre was performing in front of them every night. Houdini, however, denied supernatural powers. Once, after escaping the can, he informed the audience that the escape involved nothing supernatural. He added that he always endeavoured to be 'as honest as possible with the public'. His denial of supernatural agency reinforced the message that his feats were a product of skill rather than magic.

He was sure to claim originality for the escape. He complained to the audience that it had been performed in Sydney the year before as 'Tommy Burns' milk can'. Houdini told the crowd that he felt he owed them an explanation. In fact, the original handcuff king had not patented the milk can escape in Australia and thus had no power to prevent the imitators. Knowing Houdini's dislike of them, and his desire to be original, this fact must have been extremely upsetting. His approach to Tommy Burns was typical and recalled his approach to both Sceptic and the committee man in Melbourne. Houdini made a public announcement in the theatre condemning the imitator. He confronted the problem head on and asserted the fact that he was the originator of the escape.

The milk can escape was introduced two weeks into Houdini's run in Sydney. In Melbourne he had waited three weeks to introduce it. The Sydney press thought that the milk can escape was more impressive than Metamorphosis, and perhaps it was their initial scepticism that caused Houdini to introduce it earlier to the act.

The week 2 April to 8 April 1910 began with large crowds at Houdini performances. It ended with the introduction of the milk can escape, continued large crowds and a warmer attitude from the press. It was overall a successful week.

The dive into the Dom Baths

Houdini, despite the doubts about sharks expressed to the Adelaide press, seemed eager to perform a dive in every Australian city in which he performed. Thus he organised an underwater escape in Sydney.

The advertisements for this escape emphasised its death-defying nature, thus creating an element of excitement for the crowd. The spectators were encouraged to consider the possibilities of Houdini's survival, rather than speculating upon the manner of his release.

On Monday 11 April, advertisements began appearing in the Sydney press:

> Daring Dive
> Houdini the world famous escapologist will appear at the municipal baths on Thursday next April 14th at 1.30pm prompt.

It continued by stating that Houdini would have his arms handcuffed behind his back, his elbows secured to his sides with heavy leg irons and a chain padlocked to a manacle encircling his neck. In addition it said that Houdini 'in this helpless condition' would be dragged to the bottom of the pool by the weight of the irons, 'making it impossible for him to rise to the surface until he has released himself'. The entrance fee was set at one shilling and patrons were reminded that Houdini appeared at every performance at Mr Harry Rickards's Tivoli theatre.

Here in true theatrical tradition was an advertisement for a great event that would thrill Sydney. Unlike the performance in Melbourne, the people of Sydney were charged to see the 'daring dive'. Not only would this have ensured that money was made from the event, but it could also have been a way to control the crowd. This desire for control over crowds was typical of an era when fear of the mob was ever present.

The municipal baths were almost certainly the 'Dom' or Domain Baths. They existed on a site that reputedly had been used for bathing, as opposed to swimming, for many years. Although retaining the name 'baths', these facilities were designed more for competitive and recreational swimming than for bathing. This was a reflection of a change in attitude towards swimming as an activity which took place at the turn of the twentieth century The baths were located on the western side of Woolloomooloo Bay. They were an enclosed part of the harbour, near the current site of the Sydney Opera House, and had been extensively renovated and almost totally rebuilt in 1908. The site was very close to the current site of the Andrew 'Boy' Charlton swimming pool, the latter being built on a concrete platform above the harbour whereas the original pool was merely a part of the harbour walled off. In fact, it seems that remnants of the old pool still exist underneath the concrete platform. At the time of Houdini's dive, the baths featured a grandstand that could seat between 1,500 and 1,700 spectators and a six-tier diving tower.

Houdini's choice of the baths for his daring dive was influenced by his fear of sharks. This fear was mentioned by the Sydney press and had been previously mentioned by the Adelaide papers. Houdini stated that he would have preferred a harbour dive, but fear of sharks made him choose the pool. It seemed strange that a man who had constantly risked his life, not least by flying in the unstable Voisin biplane, would be afraid of sharks. Houdini planned to do the jump from the second tier of the tower, said to be thirty feet (9.14 metres) high into a mere eighteen feet (5.49 metres) of water.

As the day dawned, Sydneysiders gathered outside the gates to the Domain baths waiting for them to open. Some had already bought their tickets from Palings or the Tivoli theatre. Some were waiting to buy at the gate. The gates opened at 12.30 p.m. and a large crowd, each one shilling poorer, poured into the baths. The dive was scheduled for 1.30 p.m. and just before that hour Houdini arrived. Harry Rickards and his brother John Leete may already have been surveying the crowd from the platform when Houdini made his entrance. Members of the press mingled with Houdini's assistants and the man himself stood amongst them, calm and serene.

Harry wore a tight-fitting blue costume that covered him neck to thigh. A little like a longer one-piece bathing suit of today. He was barefoot and intense as his assistants, including one *The Daily Telegraph* called Hans, secured him. According to *The Daily Telegraph*,

> Handcuffs and chains were fitted on his arms and around his neck. A pair of 'darbies' was attached to his wrist. These in turn were connected with a neck chain from behind.

In a profile picture taken just before he was about to spring from the platform, Houdini looks composed and tense. A chain is roped around his neck and he bows his head, as if at prayer. The outlines of his leg and stomach muscles are bunched, as if he was a tiger ready to leap upon its prey.

Houdini stood tall with the restraints upon him. He stood on the platform above the crowd for a long moment and took a deep breath. He stood long enough for photographers to catch the moment, in profile, for eternity. Then he turned and said dramatically, 'If I don't come up out of the water within two minutes, dive for me.' He then leapt off the tower to the pool below. With his legs wide, arms tightly clasped behind him, head bent forward and muscles bunched, he leapt into the cold water of Sydney Harbour. He leapt into it head first.

The Sydney Mail and Daily Telegraph, who covered the dive extensively, with accompanying photos, compared Houdini to a boxer or expert swimmer. *The Telegraph* extended the sporting analogy and stated that it was 'odds on' that Houdini could not escape the bonds.

Houdini dived, and forty-four seconds later he emerged triumphant from the bottom of the pool. The manacles were held above his head. He swam to the middle of the pool and was greeted by loud applause and cheering when he reached the platform. He probably acknowledged the cheers with a curt bow He had also, due to diving head first into the water, injured himself. He suffered two black eyes and the loss of several teeth, a fact not mentioned in the press coverage of the time. This injury may have been due to the fear of sharks intimidating him when he performed the dive, or it just may have been a miscalculation of some sort. Despite this, Houdini had triumphed.

The Daily Telegraph correspondent was ecstatic over the magnificent feat, although he suspected that Houdini had started to untie his bonds before reaching the water. Despite this, the paper called Houdini 'a clever performer in the branch to which he has allied himself'.

The occasion was described by the papers as a matinee. In fact, it did have many features of a theatrical performance. The dramatic introduction, the stage-managed pause for breath before the leap, the large crowds and the use of the water as a curtain to disguise the means of escape. It also had the entrance fee, the danger and sporting appeal.

Indeed, Houdini's feats were increasingly looked upon as a sport by the press. He was referred to as an athlete and compared to one repeatedly. By this stage of the tour, it was clear that his act was regarded as one of physical skill as opposed to magic. Indeed, it was this aspect of the act that seemed to appeal to the public, especially to an Australian public who considered sport almost a religion.

The dive also had a more gruesome appeal, the risk factor. The 'will he survive' aspect of the event also played a large part in attracting an audience. The advertising of the dive reinforced this message. The press also sent this message. *The Daily Telegraph* coverage was titled 'Juggling with fate'.

The sporting, physical and ghoulish aspect of Houdini's feats may have been part of the appeal, as also may have been a love of gambling and speculation. But there may have been a more subconscious motive working in the minds of those who watched Houdini escape the murky polluted depths of Sydney Harbour. Many of the spectators that day were themselves a mere generation or two away from chains and chain gangs. Perhaps Houdini's daring feat appealed to some subconscious desire in their hearts to escape the shackles that a convict heritage brought to them. Or perhaps the sight of Houdini standing above the crowd in chains and manacles evoked images of ancestors who trudged ashore at Sydney Harbour a mere one hundred and twenty-two years before.

The Sydney challenges

At the conclusion of his Saturday 2 April performance, Houdini announced that he would begin taking challenges the following week. He added that he would not accept a challenge unless the challenger was named. This was probably due to his earlier problems with sceptic and *The Age* newspaper in Melbourne. In Sydney, at least three challenges met this criterion.

On Wednesday 13 April, *The Sydney Morning Herald* carried an advertisement for a challenge to Houdini. Three gentlemen of Sydney,

Messrs John Anderson, James Williamson and William Elphinstone, who also provided addresses, had challenged Houdini. Their challenge was on behalf of Messrs E. Thornton, contractors and builders of Castlereagh Street, Sydney. The three men were expert carpenters and joiners.

The challenge was simple. They offered to construct a large packing case of timber. Houdini was to be sealed inside it. The box was to be secured with three-inch nails and then tied with rope. The gentlemen challenged Houdini to escape from the box without damaging it. In the advertisement they claimed 'that it will be impossible for him to escape'. A broadsheet was published with the details of the challenge and given to passersby in the city.

There were certain conditions attached to the challenge. Whilst there was no objection to Houdini inspecting the box before the escape, the challengers demanded the right to inspect it immediately prior to the performance. The box was placed in the vestibule of the Tivoli theatre and the public was invited to inspect it. The escape was planned for the evening show of Friday 15 April.

At the appointed time, Houdini came on stage. The packing case was brought from the front of the theatre and Houdini made a speech. He stated that owing to the time that would be taken in this escape, he would cut the rest of the program. His three uniformed attendants and the curtain he used for Metamorphosis were also on stage.

Houdini added that this escape was not due to supernatural agency. He read the challenge aloud. He then invited the carpenters and a committee of twenty audience members onto the stage. The challengers commenced to re-nail the box and several nails were put in askew. Houdini jumped into the box and the final nails were driven into the timber. Before he was finally sealed within, the box was tilted so that the audience could see that he was still there. The box was roped and the curtain placed around it.

It took eleven minutes for Houdini to escape. During that time the band played 'rather loudly'. The curtain was bumped and the audience immediately focused their attention on stage, where Houdini stepped out in front of the curtain. He was described as 'calm and unruffled', but coatless. The audience cheered and Houdini left the stage with a bow. The box was once again displayed at the front of the theatre and the audience looked upon it with perplexed expressions as they left for the night.

The newspapers briefly recorded Houdini's success with this escape and stated that he was looking for further challenges. He did not have long to wait.

The next challenge was published in the *Herald* and the *Daily Telegraph* on Wednesday 20 April. The challenge came from a group of self-described hospital and lunacy attendants. Messrs Clarke, Gibson, and Woolwright had worked at various asylums and hospitals around Sydney.

The particulars of the challenge were quite detailed:

1st. They will bandage his hands to his sides

2nd. They will roll him in a number of large sheets in mummy fashion

3rd. They will fasten him down to an iron hospital bed with strong linen bandages

4th. They will pour from 10 to 15 buckets of water over his form, so as to cause all the materials and knots to shrink, holding him in a positively helpless condition

5th. The attempt to escape to take place in full view of the audience.

The last condition demonstrated a sense of scepticism from the lunacy attendants, although in the preamble of the challenge the men stated that Houdini's escapes had been 'marvellous'.

Unlike the fairly detailed coverage of the challenges by the Melbourne press, the Sydney papers were restrained in their reports. Houdini attempted this challenge on 22 April. The only major paper that carried a report of this escape was the *Town and Country Journal*, not noted for its Houdini coverage. *The Magic Mirror*, the journal of

The Australian Society of Magicians, also carried a report of the escape. Their interest was obviously professional. The mass-distributed papers merely noted that Houdini had successfully escaped the challenge.

Houdini came to the stage for this challenge dressed in his famous blue swimming costume. One of the challengers objected to this garb, so the escapologist duly exited the stage and changed into pants. He was wrapped up in calico bandages by the challengers. They then lashed him to a hospital bed. Four buckets of water were poured over him, and for twenty minutes he struggled and strained with apparently no result. He called for a drink and renewed his efforts. He firstly got his feet out of the bottom bandage and his knees above the second one. He then freed his hands and used them to pull the sheets and sit up in the bed. He escaped the remaining bandages and rolled to the floor, still bound by sheets. At this stage, one of the challengers offered to help him. He refused the offer and finally rolled himself free of the sheets. It had taken him thirty-five minutes to get free. According to *The Magic Mirror*, 'he appeared very tired' after the effort. The magazine also offered this comment:

> The ASM (Australian Society of Magicians) was well represented both on the stage and in the audience.

Which left the intriguing possibility that the ASM may have been more involved in the escapes than was recognised.

The third challenge was issued on the next Wednesday 27 April. It originated from Mr James McGrath, saddler and harness maker of Rawson Place. Mr McGrath challenged Houdini to escape from a large sleeved canvas bag. He would use strong leather straps and belting to secure Houdini's arms. He added,

> Instead of the bag going over your head it will be made to fit around your shoulders, being held into position by a broad leather strap encircling your neck.

The bag was designed to cover Houdini from his neck to his feet. Mr McGrath asked for two days' notice so that he could construct the restraint. He also added two conditions. The escape was to take place in full view of the audience and no assistance was to be given to Houdini. 'Houdini has accepted the challenge' screamed the advertisement in *The Daily Telegraph*.

The predicament forced upon Houdini sounded very uncomfortable and difficult. It seemed designed to combat Houdini's trick of dislocating his shoulders. It was issued after Houdini had given the interview where he revealed this secret.

Houdini attempted to escape this contraption during his last Friday evening performance in Australia, 29 April. *The Daily Telegraph* gave a brief description of the escape the next day. Houdini firstly freed his feet from the belting. He passed his arms beneath his feet and thus manoeuvred them to the back of his body. He was then able to open the straps at the back and free himself from the restraint.

These were the only three challenges accepted by Houdini in Sydney and they were all carefully organised. As in Melbourne they were advertised from the Wednesday through to the Friday of the performance. They were attempted on the Friday evening performance over three successive weeks.

Houdini had time to prepare for the challenges and it was his preparation that ensured the successful escapes. The challenges were a way to freshen the act. They made it different every Friday night, as they were the only feat performed on stage. Their unpredictability attracted large crowds and may have brought people back to the act for a second or third time. They were also great publicity for the ultimate showman, and for the theatre.

They also drew attention to Houdini's other daring feat, flying in the Voisin biplane.

Flying in Sydney

On Sunday 17 April, Houdini began his aviation trials in Sydney. The location of the trials was Rosehill Racecourse, to the west of Sydney near Parramatta. The racecourse, as the name implies, was a field for horse racing. It is still in use today. There does not seem to be any acknowledgment of Houdini's feats at the location.

Hundreds of people gathered on 17 April to see Houdini fly. Unfortunately, due to wind, the trials were abandoned and the people went home disappointed.

On Monday 18 April, Houdini tried again. A small group of spectators which quickly built to a larger group watched him make three attempts at flight. The attempts were delayed by the necessity to train horses. The priority for most Australians was sport rather than history.

It was a cold and windless morning. As Houdini waited for final preparations to be made, he smoked a cigarette. This was highly unusual for Houdini, and it indicated that he was nervous. He gave orders in a 'quiet yet incisive manner', and watched with a 'critical though quite unmoved eye'.

At approximately 8 a.m. he took off and made a flight lasting between three to four minutes which covered a few hundred metres. This marked the first officially recorded successful powered, controlled flight in New South Wales.

As the crowd slowly grew in size, Houdini made a second attempt. Unfortunately the plane refused to rise after taxiing along the runway. On the third attempt, the plane hopped, then finally rose to the air. It turned right, then left and descended. It lurched sharply to the left as it did so and landed with a thud. Houdini was thrown from the aircraft. He fell to his hands and knees nearby, shaken but uninjured.

On Tuesday 19 April, Houdini again attempted to fly. These flights were measured and recorded by Mr George Augustine Taylor, the honorary secretary of the Aerial League of Australia. During the flights of 19 April, Houdini reportedly reached a height of about fifty feet (15.24 metres). The wind interfered with his aircraft and the flight attempts were not as spectacular as those of the previous day. The landings, however, were smoother. A newspaper report described the landing as a 'gentle upward glide, followed by a poise, and then an easy settling on the ground'. This indicated that Houdini was becoming more comfortable and skilled with piloting. Once again there were spectators who held gamely to their hats as the plane's propellers began to turn. They pressed forward excitedly as the plane warmed up and looked up in wonder as Houdini flew around them.

The flights at Rosehill on 18–19 April received extensive press coverage. *The Sydney Mail* devoted a full page including photographs to the event, *The Daily Telegraph* had a half page and for the first time *The Sydney Morning Herald* put Houdini in the news pages as opposed to the amusement columns. In fact, news of his flights made the front-page news summary of the paper. Houdini's flights in Sydney were being recognised as significant events in the life of the city.

Perhaps encouraged by the press coverage, Houdini or Rickards decided to advertise and promote flying exhibitions. The next week, advertisements began appearing in the press for Houdini's flying exhibitions. The first advertisement appeared on 25 April. Dubbed 'Aviation week at Rosehill Racecourse', the advertisement read like an announcement of a show:

> Mr Harry Rickards at enormous expense has arranged with the great Houdini to give a series of public flights on his Voisin Biplane.

The cost of admission was one shilling.

It was clear that Houdini thought there was money to be made. He would have been encouraged in this idea by the number of people watching the flights the previous week. To make attendance easier for the public, train timetables were printed with the advertisement. Broadsheets were given to passersby on the streets of Sydney.

The flights were advertised to take place between 9 a.m. and 12 noon, weather permitting. Unfortunately the weather was not suitable for flying on 25 April, so the exhibition was cancelled due to high winds.

Another advertisement to the same effect was placed in the *Herald* on 26 April. The hours of the exhibition were changed to 9 a.m. to 3 p.m. Admission remained at one shilling. Mrs Houdini was also advertised as making tea for the event. This was probably to ensure that those who attended were not disappointed if the flight did not occur.

After 26 April, there were no more advertisements. Whether the winds, lack of interest by the public and Houdini or other factors were involved is unknown. The other possibility is that Houdini, who was finishing his season at the Tivoli, had no more need of publicity. Therefore the public flight exhibitions were no longer necessary.

On Friday 29 April, The Aerial League of NSW gave an aviation demonstration at the Sydney Town Hall. It was titled 'What the world is doing in Aerial conquest'. The exhibition included model aeroplanes and a showing of film of Houdini's flight at Diggers Rest. The invitation also stated that Houdini would be presented with the League's trophy. Admission was one shilling.

The trophy was a fine piece of workmanship. A picture was published in *The Daily Telegraph* of 3 May. Mr Gilbert Doble had sculptured it at three days' notice. The inscription on it read,

> The Aerial League of Australia, to H. Houdini, for the first aerial flight in Australia March 16th 1910.

The inscription pointedly ignored the claims of Custance and other pretenders. It officially recognised Houdini as the first flier in Australia. The date inscribed on it was 16 March, although Houdini's first flight at Diggers Rest did not take place until 18 March. Custance had flown on 17th, so the date on the trophy ensured that Houdini's claims were justified. It has been suggested that the date was engraved upon the trophy by Houdini to bolster his claims of being Australia's first aviator.

On Sunday 1st May, Houdini made his last flights in Australia. He was successful with at least one of these. Men tossed their hats and women wept in excitement as he flew. They mobbed the plane as he landed. Houdini made a speech to mark the occasion.

The Daily Telegraph printed a remarkable photograph of the day. Harry in white or light-coloured loose shirt, arms clasped behind his back, stands slightly hunched forward, his neck, arm and shoulder muscles bulging. He is surrounded by about twenty young men, including G.A. Taylor, Mr Brassac and Mr G.C. Hamilton; the Voisin looms in the background. Houdini does not look at the camera, he looks to his right. He is not at the centre of the group, but the focus of the photo is upon him, as the whole group leans towards him. It is as if all the surrounding men are drawn towards the exciting American by an invisible magnetism, a charisma that shines through the old photograph. Houdini looks disdainful, as if ignoring the photographer and the surrounding admirers. It is a strange and wonderful snapshot of a famous moment in time. It was also a fitting farewell to Sydney by a man who had drawn so much excitement and attention to himself.

Farewell

On 3 May, Houdini visited Rosehill and watched as his biplane was dismantled and packed into boxes for the trip to the northern hemisphere. He had finished his season at the Tivoli and was preparing for a return to the United States. He intended to return via Queensland.

Houdini probably travelled via train north to Brisbane. He arrived in Queensland via an overland route on 10 May. The press did not record his precise movements at the time. Houdini discussion in the papers was confined to his aviation feats and their impact on Australia.

Houdini, Bess, his assistants, and Brassac were due to leave Brisbane on 11 May. They were travelling via the steamer *The Manuka*. Before leaving Australia, Houdini spent some time with Harry Rickards. They tossed a coin for £30 towards the cost of a berth. Houdini won the toss and Rickards became £30 poorer. It was a small price to pay for the profit the theatre owner had made during the tour. On 11 May the steamer, carrying the most famous escapologist in the world, left Australia.

On 15 June 1910, *The Magic Mirror* published a note that the Australian Society of Magicians had received from Houdini. It was dated 17 May, from Suva, Fiji. The note read,

> Arrived safe so far. Have only been sick one day; a record for Houdini. Boat packed full – I always was a good draw!!
> Regards to all
> HARRY HOUDINI
> (Australia's first aviator)

It was Houdini's farewell to Australia.

Sources

Arrival
Kenneth Silverman, *Houdini!!! The Career of Erich Weiss*
The Magic Mirror Vol. II No. 2 15/2/1910
The Adelaide Advertiser 7/2/1910

Melbourne
The Magic Mirror Vol. II No. 2 15/4/1910, Vol. II No, 9 15/9/1910
Ruth Brandon, *The Lives and Many Deaths of Harry Houdini*
The Argus 7/2/1910

First performance in Melbourne
Richard Waterhouse, *From Minstrel Show to Vaudeville: The Australian Popular Stage 1788–1914*
The Argus 7/2/1910
New Opera House Theatre Programme Feb.–March 1910, courtesy of Gerald Taylor
Sydney Morning Herald 29/3/1910
The Age 8/2/1910

The committee man
The Age, *The Argus* 14/2/1910
Silverman op. cit.

The Yarra dive
Advertisements in the *The Age* and *The Argus* 16/2, 18/2/1910
The Age 17/2, 18/2/1910
The Magic Mirror Vol. II No. 9 15/9/1910

Milk can escape
Advertisements *The Age* and *The Argus* 14/2/1910
General details from Silverman op. cit. and Brandon op. cit.
The Argus 28/2, 10/3/1910
The Age 10/3/1910
Charles Waller, *Magical Nights in the Theatre*

The Melbourne challenges
Advertisements in *The Age* 10/2, 24/2, 2/3, 4/3/1910 and in *The Argus* 16/2/1910
The Argus 12/2/1910
The Age 4/2, 4/3/1910
The Weekly Times, 12/2, 19/2/1910
Waller op. cit.

Sceptic
The Age 11/3, 12/3/1910
The Argus 10/3/1910

First flight
Background details from Charles Harvard Gibbs-Smith, *Aviation An Historical Survey from its Origins to the End of WWII*
The Pioneers saluting the men & women of aviation history website by Russell Naughton http://www.ctie.monash.edu.au/hargrave/houdini bio.html
The Age 18/3, 19/3/1910
The Argus 19/3, 21/3, 23/3/1910
The Australasian 26/6/1910, 'Aeroplane Flights in Australia'
Correspondence from La Trobe Librarian to unknown correspondent 19/11/1981

Houdini's arrival in Sydney

Theatre magazine, September 1909
The Referee 4/7/1917, 2/3/1910
Sydney Morning Herald 28/3, 26/3/1910

The Sydney performance

Sydney Morning Herald 26/3, 29/3/1910
The Daily Telegraph 29/3/1910
Tivoli Sydney Theatre Programme March 1910
Brandon op. cit.
Sydney Mail 30/3/1910

Autumn in Sydney

The Daily Telegraph 4/4, 11/4, 16/4/1910
The Referee 6/4, 13/4/1910
The Sydney Mail 13/4/1910

The Dive into the Dom Baths

Sydney Morning Herald 11/4/1910
Sydney Mail 20/4/1910

Daily Telegraph 11/4, 15/4/1910
Silverman op. cit.

The Sydney challenges

The Sydney Morning Herald 4/4, 13/4, 20/4, 29/4/1910
Magic Mirror Vol. II No. 5 15/5/1910
Daily Telegraph 29/4/1910
The Town and Country Journal 27/4/1910

Flying

Sydney Morning Herald 19/4, 25/4, 29/4/1910
The Daily Telegraph 20/4/1910
The Sydney Mail 20/4/1910
Silverman op. cit.

Farewell

The Courier Mail 11/5/1910
Sydney Morning Herald 9/5/1910
Magic Mirror Vol. II No. 6, 15/6/1910
Silverman op. cit.

Bibliography

Books

Brandon, Ruth, *The Lives and Many Deaths of Harry Houdini*, Pan Books, London, 2000.

Gibbs-Smith, Charles Harvard, *Aviation: An Historical Survey from its Origins to the End of WWII*, HMSO, London, 1970.

Silverman, Kenneth, *Houdini!!! The Career of Erich Weiss*, Harper Collins, New York, 1996.

Waterhouse, Richard, *From Minstrel Show to Vaudeville. The Australian Popular Stage 1788–1914*, University of NSW Press, Kensington NSW, 1990.

Waller, Charles, *Magical Nights at the Theatre*, edited and published by Gerald Taylor, Melbourne, 1980.

Newspapers

The Sydney Morning Herald
The Daily Telegraph
The Age
The Argus
The Sydney Mail
The Referee
The Town and Country Journal
The Magic Mirror

Ephemera

New Opera House Theatre Programme Feb.–March 1910, courtesy of Gerald Taylor.

Tivoli Sydney Programme March–April 1910.

www.ingramcontent.com/pod-product-compliance
Lightning Source LLC
Chambersburg PA
CBHW030916080526
44589CB00010B/330